EXTREME CAREERS

VOLCANOLOGISTS
Life Exploring Volcanoes

Chris Hayhurst

the rosen publishing group's
rosen
central

Published in 2003 by The Rosen Publishing Group, Inc.
29 East 21st Street, New York, NY 10010

First Edition

Library of Congress Cataloging-in-Publication Data

Hayhurst, Chris.
Volcanologists: life exploring volcanoes / Chris Hayhurst.— 1st ed.
p. cm. — (Extreme careers)
Includes bibliographical references and index.
ISBN 0-8239-3637-6 (library binding)
1. Volcanological research—Juvenile literature. 2.
Volcanologists—Juvenile literature. [1. Volcanologists. 2. Volcanoes.
3. Occupations.] I. Title. II. Series.
QE521.3 .H29 2003
551.21'07'2—dc21

                                                    2001006284

Manufactured in the United States of America

Contents

"It's Hot Out There!"

Perhaps you have already thought about what you would like to do when you're older. Maybe you want to become a police officer, a teacher, a scientist, or a professional athlete. Or maybe you'll start your own business. You might want to follow in the footsteps of a parent or other close relative, or maybe you'll invent an entirely new career. While a lot of people have office jobs, others prefer careers that might be called "extreme," like race car driving, working as a secret agent, exploring the seas as a professional scuba diver, or fighting fires with the local fire department. These jobs require tremendous skill, training, and ambition. They can also be dangerous. Picture swimming to the bottom of the ocean with nothing

4

but a metal tank strapped to your back to keep you alive. Or imagine your fear—and excitement—as you rush into a burning house to rescue a trapped child.

Some careers—like that of a volcanologist, a scientist who studies volcanoes—are challenging both in the office and out in the field. You might spend entire weeks or even months in the laboratory or in front of a computer reading through professional journals, writing reports, and discussing results with your colleagues. You'll give the occasional presentation to other professional volcanologists and spend a good deal of time listening to what they have to say as well.

However, fieldwork is the aspect of volcanology that many scientists enjoy the most. Volcanologists often spend time hiking up steep volcanoes, being lowered down into craters, and conducting research right on site. For the most part, this work is uneventful. Tests are run, data is collected, everyone enjoys the great views, and then it's back to the lab where the results can be analyzed. But sometimes things aren't quite so straightforward. Active volcanoes can "blow" at any time.

Volcanology is not for crazy scientists who don't value their lives. The truth is, if you know what

The Legend of Vulcan

The word "volcano" comes from the name the ancient Romans gave to their god of fire and metalworking, Vulcan. According to legend, Vulcan (known as Hephaestus to the ancient Greeks) hammered away at rocks deep beneath the earth as he labored to make weapons for other gods. Occasionally, he worked with so much force that fire, boulders, and lava would explode out of the ground and into the sky. What we know as a volcanic eruption, the ancient Romans believed to be a sign from the gods.

you're doing and you receive the right training, volcanology is actually quite safe. Like any extreme career, you just have to go about your job in the way you know best. Risk comes with the territory, but if you do things right, those risks can be minimized.

As you read this book, consider what it takes to become a volcanologist. If the job sounds appealing, use the resources in the back of the book to get more information and start making plans. Then, when you're old enough to go to college and get a job, dive right in. Remember, you don't need to decide what you want to be just yet. You're young. There's plenty of time. But it never hurts to dream. And if you dream of becoming a volcanologist, well, you never know—somewhere there just might be a volcano with your name on it.

The Danger Zone

1

Most volcanoes are like enormous, hibernating animals. They do absolutely nothing. They sit there like any other mountain, day after day, year after year. Volcanoes come in all shapes and sizes—big, small, steep slopes, gradual slopes. Some are giant, rounded, mound-shaped hills. Others are hidden under vast and beautiful lakes. Still others are found deep beneath the ocean. People swim and sail in these lakes, hike and climb these hills and mountains, and snorkel and scuba dive these ocean waters without any idea that they're even near a volcano.

Volcanoes are found all over the world, sometimes in places you would least expect them. There are volcanoes in Mexico and throughout Central America.

There are volcanoes in the United States and Canada. There are also volcanoes in New Zealand, Tanzania, Ireland, and India, just to name a few places. Hundreds of millions of people live near these volcanoes or even on them, and many of those people don't even know what a volcano is.

For the most part, people who live on or near a volcano have nothing to fear. The great majority of volcanoes will never erupt in a person's lifetime. And as long as there are no eruptions, most volcanoes are no

Millions of people worldwide, like these rice farmers near the Mayon volcano in the Philippines, live in close proximity to volcanoes.

Volcanologists: Life Exploring Volcanoes

Major Cascade Range Volcanoes

Mount Baker
Glacier Peak
WASHINGTON
Seattle
Mount Rainier
Mount St. Helens
Mount Adams
Portland
Mount Hood
Mount Jefferson
Three Sisters
OREGON
Newberry Volcano
Crater Lake (Mount Mazama)
Mount McLoughlin
Medicine Lake Volcano
Mount Shasta
CALIFORNIA
Lassen Peak
NEVADA
BRITISH COLUMBIA
PACIFIC OCEAN

0   100
Miles

USGS

Topinka, USGS/CVO, 1997, Modified from: Tilling, et al., 1990

The Cascades are a volcanic range that extend from northern California to British Columbia.

more dangerous than an average mountain. The problem, of course, is that volcanoes do erupt sometimes, and when they do, they can be deadly. It's when a volcano wakes up and erupts that people suddenly take notice of the monster at their door.

Living on the Edge

The Pacific Northwest region of the United States has a lot going for it. Cities like Seattle, Washington, and Portland, Oregon, are thriving. Residents love the urban culture, as well as the easy access to the ocean and nearby mountains. It's a beautiful part of the world. One of the main draws to the area is the Cascade Range, a breathtaking chain of mountains stretching from northern California up across the border into Canada. For the average hiker or climber, the Cascades offer an endless assortment of peaks, valleys, rivers, and forests that are ideal for exploring. These mountains are a great getaway—a fantastic place to escape from everyday life and enjoy nature.

In the early 1980s, however, the truth behind the Cascades suddenly became all too apparent. Most people in the Pacific Northwest knew that the region was littered with volcanoes, but to them, volcanism was something of the geological past. Yes, there had been many eruptions in the area over the last several thousand years, but that didn't matter. The likelihood of an eruption in modern times was so slim that it wasn't worth worrying about. However, volcanologists were convinced otherwise, and some did worry. In their opinion, the Cascades were home to dozens of potentially active—and deadly—volcanoes. By

Fact

The tallest volcano in the continental United States is the 14,411-foot Mount Rainier, located ninety miles south of Seattle, Washington.

The catastrophic and unexpected eruption of Mount St. Helens in Washington State in May 1980 killed fifty-seven people.

studying the area, the volcanologists determined that, in the region, an average of two eruptions occurred every hundred years. These volcanoes were sleeping, but they were anything but dead.

Mount St. Helens

In the early spring of 1980, the volcanologists' fears became a reality. Suddenly, the 8,364-foot Mount St. Helens in southwest Washington—near Portland and the Oregon border—began experiencing earthquakes and minor eruptions. According to the scientists' gauges, it didn't look good. This volcano, at least, had finally woken up. Scientists quickly warned local officials and put the word out that an evacuation of the area was necessary. Most nearby residents gathered their belongings and fled. Some stayed, however, refusing to believe that an eruption would occur and gambling that even if one did take place, it was highly unlikely to affect them. Then, on May 18, 1980, Mount St. Helens erupted.

The tremendous explosion sent massive clouds of hot gas and dust into the air and blasted the entire summit into the sky. When the smoke finally cleared, fifty-seven people had died. Nearby communities suffered more than $1 billion in damages. People around the country—and the world—were shocked. A volcano? In the United States? So close to a city and so many people? Millions of Pacific Northwest residents suddenly had to face a harsh reality: These were real-life volcanoes in their backyards—real-life volcanoes that could erupt at any time. They were dangerous, and they were here to stay.

FACT

The David A. Johnson Cascades Volcano Observatory, located in Vancouver, Washington, was named for a scientist of the United States Geological Observatory who was killed in the May 18, 1980, eruption of Mount St. Helens. He was working when he was killed, observing the volcano for signs of danger.

Monitoring Volcanoes

Despite the eruption of Mount St. Helens, people continue to pour into the Pacific Northwest. Houses are being built closer and closer to the Cascades, and, it appears, few people seem to care. Volcanologists, however, are taking this population

Large windows at the Johnson Ridge Observatory give a
breathtaking view of Mount St. Helens years after its eruption.

growth seriously. They know that with more people in
the region there is an increased danger of catastrophe
in the event of an eruption. To help lessen this risk,
scientists from the United States Geological Survey
(USGS) built a volcano observatory in the area following the Mount St. Helens eruption. From there they
can monitor the region's volcanoes and keep tabs on
developing hazards.

    With the aid of the observatory, scientists hoped to
be able to watch all the volcanoes in the Cascade

Volcanologists: Life Exploring Volcanoes

Range. However, they soon realized that it was impossible for one observatory to monitor all of the region's volcanoes. There were just too many. To fix this problem and enable them to study a variety of volcanoes all over the United States (including the Pacific Northwest, eastern California, Wyoming, Alaska, and Hawaii) and the world, the USGS turned to portable monitoring devices that allowed them to bring their gear to whatever volcano they wished to study.

In the Pacific Northwest, scientists use numerous earthquake sensors to detect seismic activity at volcanoes. When they detect activity indicating that an eruption could occur, scientists at the Cascades Volcano Observatory rush their portable equipment to the volcano in question and do more extensive testing. If the situation is dangerous, local officials are alerted and the area is evacuated. However, as there have not been any major eruptions in the Cascades since Mount St. Helens, evacuations have not been necessary.

Scientists at the observatory have also done many studies of the geological history of the area. This helps determine the possibility of long-term hazards such as landslides or mudslides, which often occur even when there are no eruptions. The data they

Willie Scott of the USGS Cascades Volcano Observatory in Vancouver, Washington, points to seismographic readings from an earthquake that hit Seattle in 2001. It was the strongest to hit in decades.

collect is used by local officials to determine where it is safe for people to live in the area.

Mount Rainier

One particularly dangerous volcano is 14,411-foot Mount Rainier, located outside of Seattle, Washington. Parts of suburban Seattle are actually situated right near the volcano, with houses and other structures built directly on top of deposits of volcanic ash. The

Volcano Zone

In the last several thousand years, there have been more than 1,000 eruptions in the Cascade Range of the Pacific Northwest. While many of these eruptions were fairly minor, some were extremely explosive. Historically, Cascade eruptions have been very violent. They've sent avalanches of ash and rock—called pyroclastic flows—crashing down steep slopes, and have produced lava flows and landslides that destroyed everything in their path. They've also sent massive mudflows, called lahars, down into valleys far away from the eruption zone, as well as giant clouds of ash high into the sky. The Cascade volcanoes might not be so dangerous if no one lived in the area, but that is not the case, and people still continue to relocate to this beautiful region year after year.

In all, there are thirteen volcanoes in the Cascades that could erupt at any time. You may have heard of some of them—Mount Hood, Mount Adams, Mount Jefferson, and Mount St. Helens are just a few. According to the USGS Cascades Volcano Observatory, eleven of these volcanoes have erupted in the last 4,000 years. Seven have erupted in the last 200 years. More than 100 eruptions have taken place in the range over the last 4,000 years. Scientists consider these volcanoes to be some of the most dangerous in the United States.

peak has erupted at least four times and has produced many lahars in the last 4,000 years. Rainier is particularly prone to landslides and lahars because there is a lot of glacier ice at its higher elevations. The heat from an eruption melts the ice, which quickly slides down the steep slopes of the volcano. Volcanologists who have studied the mountain and its surroundings have concluded that future mudflows would strike the same areas as they did in the past—and the structures that are now on them—if Rainier erupted again. For this reason, they continue to monitor Rainier and other volcanoes in the area, hoping that if an eruption occurs, they'll be able to give residents enough time to evacuate.

Volcanologist: The World's Hottest Job?

2

Volcanologists are in high demand. There are volcanoes similar to those in the Cascades—but far more dangerous—all over the world. It's absolutely necessary that scientists learn everything they can about these volcanoes in order to save lives and further our knowledge and understanding of geology. In the same way that biologists study living organisms and chemists study chemical reactions, volcanologists study the way volcanoes work. They study how volcanoes are formed. They map where volcanoes— both old ones and newly formed ones—are located around the world. They classify volcanoes based on their specific geological characteristics. They examine the structure of volcanoes as well as the various things that are ejected from them during eruptions, such as lava, gas, ash, and dust. Volcanologists incorporate other geological phenomena into their studies, too. They know that earthquakes, for example, are closely related to volcanic eruptions. By understanding earthquakes, they can tell whether a minor tremor might indicate that an eruption is coming soon.

Forecasting

One of the most important goals for a volcanologist is to figure out how to predict, or forecast, when future eruptions will take place. This allows them to be able to warn people who live in the vicinity of potentially dangerous volcanoes before they erupt. An early warning can mean the difference between life and death for thousands or even millions of people. Also, by studying volcanoes, volcanologists can learn more about the earth and its natural processes. Volcanologists study how volcanic rocks were formed, where volcanic gases are from, and how volcanic soils affect the growth of plants and the survival of the wildlife that depend on those plants.

Scientists often use sophisticated measurement techniques and equipment to track the progress of magma and lava flow in and around a volcano.

Ultimately, these scientists can learn geological details that might not be obvious to other researchers.

One way volcanologists create accurate forecasts is by studying a volcano's history and past eruptions. They do this by examining rocks and minerals in the earth, and noting the volcano's geological history. Based on this information—as well as data from people who observed past eruptions, or certain geological conditions—they can look for trends that would show when it might erupt again. The scientists note what caused these eruptions, and they examine the events that led up to them. Volcanologists also use sophisticated instruments that measure changes in the volcano's structure and the gases within it. For example, they can record slight changes in the slope of the volcano that are caused by the swelling of magma—the hot, liquid rock found deep inside the earth—beneath it. This work is similar to putting a puzzle together. The volcanologists look at all the pieces and figure out how they relate to each other. When they have the puzzle figured out, they can take what they've learned about the past and apply it to the present.

Monitoring Volcanoes

Volcanic monitoring is a way of observing volcanoes and recording their changes. It requires close observation of obvious details like how much steam a volcano emits and not-so-obvious things like the condition of plants in a volcano's immediate vicinity. While monitoring a volcano, volcanologists might take note of things like new cracks in the ground or old cracks that have gotten wider. They would look at plants to see if they're dying for reasons related to changes in the air quality. They would also look for changes in the rocks, minerals, and vapors around fumaroles on the volcano. Fumaroles are holes from which gases and materials from inside the volcano often escape.

When volcanologists determine that a long-dormant volcano may be due for an eruption, they spend lots of time and money monitoring it. It would be impossible to monitor every volcano in the world like this, so they have to pick the volcanoes that are most

Scientists install a seismic station that will measure early signs of volcanic activity close to the dome of Mount St. Helens.

likely to erupt or that present the greatest danger to local populations.

When eruptions occur, volcanologists step up their monitoring even more. They often film and record eruptions. They also take notes as they watch the eruption, jotting down significant observations from the start of the eruption to the end. They measure the temperature of erupting lava and gases as well. They collect gas and lava samples and bring them back to their labs for analysis. They measure how much lava and ash is ejected and how fast the lava travels over ground. These measurements can tell a scientist a lot about a specific volcano and about volcanoes in general. Ultimately, the data may provide valuable information for the science of volcanology.

Minding the Details

Some volcanic monitoring requires recording and analyzing information that is impossible to observe with the naked eye. For these observations, volcanologists use high-tech instruments that are capable of making precise measurements. Some instruments collect data on ground movements such as a minor earthquake that might not be felt by a person standing on the ground. Earthquakes are caused when pressure from heated and liquefied rock beneath the earth's surface forces the ground to crack. By studying the size and location of earthquakes, scientists can detect exactly where the magma beneath the surface is flowing and predict where it might go next.

This kind of buildup of pressure also leads to changes in the composition of gas. As the magma pushes upward, it often forces various gases out through cracks in the surface. Special instruments can measure these gases as they come out and compare them to gases that are usually found in the area. A major difference in gas composition might be an indication that an eruption is on the way. Other instruments are equipped with lasers that can detect even the slightest changes in the tilt of a volcano's slope. Such a change can indicate that magma is pushing up toward the surface and may be about to explode.

Slow Going

One problem volcanologists often encounter in their research is the fact that volcanoes work on geologic time. That is, volcanologists may be able to record their observations and study the previously recorded observations of other scientists, but these observations provide just a snapshot of one phase in the long life of a volcano, and not the entire picture. While most volcanoes have been around for eons, scientists don't have information that dates back far enough in time to be able to fully determine how a volcano might behave. It would be like trying to predict a person's future when you've known him or her for just five minutes—in other words, impossible.

In an attempt to zero in on this foggy geological history, scientists spend countless hours studying the evidence left behind from past eruptions. They look at the layers of ash and lava deposited over thousands of years and use complex dating techniques to figure out how old everything is. By analyzing these ancient flows, they can determine which areas surrounding a volcano are the most prone to future hazards, such as lava flows, ash fall, exposure to toxic gases, and mudflows. In effect, volcanologists work at piecing together a history of the volcano and then use that history to help get a glimpse into the future.

Preparing the Public

When a volcanologist does predict a potentially dangerous eruption, it's time to take action. He or she must immediately alert local government officials, discuss potential problems and concerns, and alert any residents of the affected area, making sure they know what to do to keep out of harm's way.

Of course, some eruptions are not so dangerous, and volcanologists usually know when a volcano is harmless. In such cases, they'll issue a warning to nearby residents, but an evacuation may not be required. If a volcanologist believes that an upcoming eruption is likely to destroy a vast area beyond the immediate slopes of the volcano, he or she will talk to local government officials and recommend that they organize an evacuation and begin emergency safety procedures.

Then, the scientists map the area and determine exactly where the danger spots are. People living in a danger zone will have to evacuate. Hospitals are notified and told to prepare for the arrival of burn victims, emergency workers are given the appropriate gear

Former Japanese prime minister, Yoshiro Mori, meets with evacuees who fled the eruption of Mount Usu in April 2000.

they need to stay safe, and people are told what they can do to help prevent damage to their homes. For instance, they can sweep ash from their roofs to prevent them from collapsing.

An alternative source of drinking water must be considered because lava and ash flows can easily pollute lakes and streams. Alternative transportation routes must also be established because flows can block roads. Large amounts of ash in the air can destroy motors, so airplanes may be forced to stay on the ground and cars may become useless.

Things can get tremendously confusing during and following an eruption. The key is in being prepared. Volcanologists play an important role in this preparation.

Safety

When you work on volcanoes, one of the most important things to consider is safety. Because a dormant, or sleeping, volcano can wake up and erupt at almost any time, volcanologists must always keep an escape route in mind. They have to be ready to evacuate, and in a real emergency, they must know exactly what to do in order to survive.

Experience counts for a lot when it comes to being safe around volcanoes. The more experience you have, the more likely it is that you'll know what to do when things get dangerous. For the most part, climbing a volcano is like climbing any other mountain. You need to be fit, wear appropriate clothing, and know how to use basic directional tools like

Volcanologists: Life Exploring Volcanoes

maps and a compass. But you also need a little extra gear. The International Association of Volcanology and Chemistry of the Earth's Interior (IAVCEI), the world's most important volcanology association, recommends that all volcanologists working on volcanoes carry the following:

◆ Handheld, two-way radios

◆ Helmets with chin straps

◆ Full-face and half-face gas masks, or respirators

◆ Goggles

◆ Brightly colored clothing suitable for protection in extreme weather conditions and from ashfall and heat

◆ Heavy boots

◆ Work gloves

◆ First-aid kits

Scientists use special equipment to collect gas samples from vents around the dome and the floor of a volcano.

◆ Water and food supplies

◆ Topographic maps, compasses, and altimeters for route finding

◆ Knives

◆ Whistles

◆ Identification tags with name, blood type, and person to contact in event of emergency

Knowing how to use this equipment is very important. After all, what good will a topographic map do you if you don't know how to read it?

Planning Saves Lives

Many volcanologists have lost their lives studying volcanoes. So many, in fact, that in 1994, following a few particularly bad years during which the death toll was especially high, geologists at the IAVCEI decided to publish a list of recommended safety precautions that they felt all volcanologists should follow. Among other things, they suggested the following:

While sampling a flow of lava during an eruption of the Kilauea volcano in Hawaii, volcanologist Christina Heliker shields herself from the extreme heat.

1. Researchers should develop a thorough safety plan before they begin work on a volcano. They should know exactly what to do in case of an emergency.

2. Researchers should leave a schedule of where they plan to be with people outside the danger zone. In the event of an emergency, this would make it easier to locate missing scientists.

3. Tourists, reporters, TV crews, and other nonscientists should not be invited to accompany volcanologists to hazardous areas.

4. Researchers should know basic first aid.
5. On high-altitude volcanoes and during winter, researchers should expect to encounter dangerous weather conditions like cold, snow, and ice, as well as avalanches, snowstorms, and other hazards.
6. Scientists should approach dangers like active craters, fumaroles, lava flows, and debris flows with extreme care and only when absolutely necessary.
7. Scientists should work quickly and efficiently and should get away from the danger zone as fast as possible.
8. Scientists should work upwind of craters and other gas-emitters (such as fumaroles) to avoid inhaling poisonous gases.
9. Scientists should stay in radio communication with experts outside the danger zone who can give a warning if their high-tech instruments indicate an eruption is about to occur.
10. Volcanologists should plan an escape route to use in an emergency.

As you can see, volcanologists do not just choose a volcano, hike up its slopes, and go to work. They spend a significant amount of time planning, preparing, packing, talking to locals, and determining what they should do in case of an emergency. Their ultimate goal is to collect data, of course, but they'd rather not lose their lives in the process. And this is only possible if safety is the first priority.

The Deadly Lahar

When it comes to volcanoes, one of the biggest hazards to people are mudflows called lahars. Such flows can travel more than a hundred miles at speeds of up to

The Volcano Disaster Assistance Program

The Volcano Disaster Assistance Program (VDAP), established in 1986, is a joint operation of the U.S. Geological Survey and the U.S. Office of Foreign Disaster Assistance. The program was designed to send volcanology experts to countries experiencing or about to experience a volcanic disaster. When a VDAP team arrives on the scene, they immediately begin working with local experts to analyze the volcano and its potential for eruption, and to help organize an emergency evacuation if necessary. In times of crises, the work of the volcanologists and other scientists who are involved with VDAP has helped save thousands of lives that may have been lost in deadly eruptions. In addition, these scientists have taken what they've learned abroad and applied that knowledge to volcanoes in the United States.

Mudflows, such as the one that damaged this home during the eruption of Mount St. Helens, are another hazard of volcanic activity.

124 miles (200 km) per hour. These are the flows that destroy entire villages and kill thousands of people. When such a flow occurs without warning, there is almost no time to escape.

Once a volcano is covered in a layer of ash, it's extremely susceptible to erosion. If hard rains come, the ash can turn into a deadly river of mud. The soaking wet ash becomes so heavy that it's no longer stable. It then flows downhill at very high speeds, building up and plucking up rocks, trees, buildings, and other man-made structures.

People saw just how deadly lahars can be in 1985 in the Colombian town of Armero, during the eruption of a volcano named Ruiz. Previous ash deposits, which were covered with snow and ice, quickly grew unstable as the ice melted and then slipped down the mountain's slope at a tremendously high speed. Armero, almost 50 miles (80 km) away, was right in the mudflow's path and was completely destroyed. More than 20,000 people died in the disaster.

The Future

Volcanology has made major strides, but it's still a relatively new science. Scientists are now able to predict eruptions in time to evacuate people who might otherwise be in danger, but there is still much more work to be done. Out of the more than 1,000 active volcanoes worldwide, relatively few are actually monitored at volcano observatories. And scientists still have no way of knowing exactly when and why a volcano will erupt. There are just too many variables that contribute to eruptions. Future volcanologists have a lot of work to do.

Using Satellites to Monitor Volcanoes

One relatively recent development in the study of volcanoes, and one that holds much promise for the future, is the use of satellites in volcanic monitoring. Scientists now use NASA satellites positioned in space to help them track eruption clouds as they move across the earth. With more and more satellites being launched into space each year, volcanologists' ability to track such clouds is improving.

This method of tracking eruption clouds is called remote sensing. The special satellites contain high-tech sensors that allow them to detect things like sulfur dioxide gas and unusual amounts of electromagnetic energy—the energy emitted during a volcanic eruption and contained in eruption clouds. This is important because vast clouds with high amounts of electromagnetic energy can disrupt electrical systems that are critical to modern technology. For instance, most airplanes would run into serious trouble if they flew into a volcanic cloud because the electromagnetic energy

Volcanologists install a satellite monitoring receiver and solar panel at the Popocatepetl volcano in the Mexican state of Puebla.

would interfere with their computers and controls. Different sensors on the satellites take various measurements of the energy in the volcanic clouds and follow them as they move. That way, people on the ground—or in the air—can be warned before eruption clouds arrive.

However, this technique is not the only way scientists track eruption clouds. Clouds can also be followed using ground-based monitoring methods. But satellite-based observation has its advantages, especially for volcanoes located in remote parts of the world where sophisticated ground-based monitoring stations have not yet been set up. The data these monitors collect ultimately give scientists valuable information they can use to learn about volcanoes, associated hazards, and the nature of eruptions.

Anatomy of an Eruption

What happens in a volcanic eruption? Here's what scientists have learned:

◆ When a volcano erupts, the magma stored beneath the earth comes to the surface as lava and volcanic gas. As the lava surges out, pockets of gas often explode and send blocks of rock out of the crater. The rock shoots up into the sky or flows downhill with the lava, which runs until it reaches flat land or a barrier that is large enough to stop it.

◆ Lava can flow downhill like a river. It can even form falls over steep drop-offs like waterfalls do. Some lava can flow at very high speeds—up to 30 miles (50 km) per hour—and can cover more than

Three Stages of an Eruption

Computer illustration of the three stages in a typical explosive volcanic eruption

When the magma (magnified directly below) reaches the surface, the pressure drop causes the gas it contains to expand explosively, blasting out lava, rocks, and a huge plume of ash.

Molten rock, or magma, rises up through weaknesses in the underlying rock.

This magma, magnified at lower right, contains small bubbles of gas (orange). As the magma rises up into the volcano, any groundwater it meets will be vaporized, increasing the pressure.

62 miles (100 km). Some flows are hundreds of yards deep. These extremely thick flows move very slowly. Others are just a few feet thick and can move much faster. Eventually, the lava begins to cool. This makes it stickier and slower. Really rough, cooled lava—sharp enough to slice your feet even with shoes on—is called "aa" lava. "Aa" is a Hawaiian word.

◆ Eruptions aren't always on land. Many take place deep under water in the ocean. This lava cools very fast and breaks into glasslike pieces.

◆ Very few lava flows actually kill people. Roads, bridges, and other man-made objects aren't so lucky, however. Lava destroys such structures quite easily and leads to millions of dollars in damage. Valuable land is often destroyed, too.

◆ Volcanic gas is mostly steam, which is water in its gaseous form, and carbon dioxide. Large amounts of carbon dioxide can be extremely dangerous. It can collect in depressions in the earth—like valleys—and poison the air, killing insects, plants, and animals, as well as people. Some gases contain other poisons, too. Fluorine, sulfur, and chlorine are all poisonous in their gaseous states, and they can kill wildlife as well. You may notice sulfur gas if you visit a hot spring. It's the rotten egg smell that makes you hold your nose.

◆ Volcanologists often go to active, erupting volcanoes to sample volcanic gases. They do this only if they are certain the eruption is relatively calm and no major explosions are about to occur. Still, because they never know exactly what is going to happen, this is risky. They put on heavy-duty protective suits to shield their bodies from the intense temperatures. They climb the volcano carefully and take many gas samples. They then bring these samples back to the laboratory where they can perform detailed experiments and determine exactly what is in the gases.

Volcanologists also take gas samples from older, solidified lava—lava that has cooled down over time and changed from a liquid to a solid. This is less dangerous because the lava—at least on the surface—is not so hot. The scientists use special techniques to "extract" gases from the rock. Gases can also be collected from hot springs, like the ones in Yellowstone National Park in Wyoming.

Volcanic Explosions

Some eruptions kick off as giant explosions. The explosion can be relatively small, like the ones that demolitionists use to knock down a building, or they may be far greater than the most powerful bombs ever built. By carefully studying solidified deposits of lava and ash, volcanologists have determined that the biggest volcanic explosions took place during ancient times, long before recorded history.

Some modern-day explosions have sent pieces of lava and gas miles straight up into the sky and into the upper atmosphere. These particles later fall back to earth hundreds of miles away from the volcano. These explosions can bury nearby villages in a matter of hours. The biggest volcanic explosions—known as ultraplinian eruptions—can scatter debris across an entire continent. These types of eruptions are extremely rare, however, and so far none have taken place during recorded history.

When magma erupts, the violent escape of gas from the lava can send millions of rock fragments into the sky. Some of those fragments fall nearby, but smaller pieces can drift away as clouds, their direction determined by the wind. When pieces fall right near the vent, they often pile up into a cone. Bigger

The fiery release of molten rock is the event most associated with a volcano's eruption.

explosions can produce huge amounts of dustlike ash, which is nothing more than pulverized rock and lava. Ash can travel for miles with the wind, eventually settling to the ground. Small amounts of ash can do wonders for soil, adding vital nutrients that help crops flourish. But large ash deposits can quickly black out the sky and suffocate and kill all kinds of plant and wildlife. These deposits can also gather on rooftops and cause buildings to collapse. They can destroy vehicles and pollute water. Eruptions can also send much larger fragments—called bombs and blocks—into the sky. If you're right near the cone of an erupting volcano, you could easily be crushed by one of these massive boulders.

An Extreme Career

How extreme a career is volcanology? Consider this: On January 14, 1993, dozens of the world's most respected volcanologists were going to meet in Pasto, Colombia, to discuss the latest techniques for studying volcanoes. They were headed for a 13,680-foot active volcano called Galeras. Here, they were going to measure temperature changes inside the volcano's cone and sample the noxious gases that spewed from its vents. The scientists hoped to collect data that would help them figure out how much of a threat the volcano was to the people of Pasto. They also hoped to predict the chances of

The flow of lava from an eruption can be slow, yet extremely deadly.

future eruptions. There had been a minor eruption the previous July, and the scientists felt that it was just a matter of time before a true catastrophe took place. However, that day, the weather was not cooperating. Clouds were looming over the city, and even in the early morning, Galeras was blanketed in thick fog. As the scientists drove to the summit, they could barely see.

Stanley Williams, a scientist from the University of Arizona, was the trip's leader. At the volcano's rim, he organized his crew. Using ropes, several scientists would go down into the cone to take gas samples. Others would remain on the rim and conduct separate experiments. Things had to move fast. An active volcano was no place for a picnic.

Disaster Strikes

For most of the day, everything went as planned. Then, without warning, at exactly 1:41 PM, the mountain began to shake. Enormous rocks that had come loose bounced down the crater's walls.

Clouds of dust rose into the sky. Williams, realizing what was happening, yelled to his colleagues. "Hurry up!" he screamed. "Get out!" Galeras was about to explode. But it was already too late. Within seconds there was an ear-splitting crack as the earth beneath the mountain split in two. A toxic, superheated blast of volcanic gases, along with hundreds of massive boulders, shot from the cone into the sky.

Everyone ran for their lives. They were lucky— everyone made it out in time.

Become a Volcanologist

There are many uncertainties when it comes to volcanology, as the field is still growing and there is still much to learn about volcanoes. Ten years from now, it is highly likely that scientists will know much more about why volcanoes erupt. They should also be able to forecast eruptions with greater accuracy.

Ultimately, the future of volcanology rests with those who decide to become volcanologists. These are the people who will break new ground and lead the way to new discoveries.

If you think volcanology might be the career you've been looking for, it's never too early to start preparing. For now, focus on doing well in school. Take every science course you can, and don't forget to hone your math and writing skills, too. When it comes time for college, you can major in geology or even volcanology if your school has a program. Then, when you graduate, you can jump right into the field. Just be sure to watch your step—it's hot out there!

Glossary

active volcano A volcano experiencing earth-quakes, movement of magma, pressure buildup, and eruptions.

altimeter An instrument for measuring altitude.

ash Fine pieces of minerals and rocks that are ejected when a volcano erupts.

catastrophe A violent and destructive natural disaster.

crater A bowl-shaped depression surrounding a volcano's opening.

dormant Not active.

eon A unit of geologic time equal to one billion years.

eruption The sudden escape of lava, gas, and ash from a volcano.

fumarole A hole on or near a volcano from which gases can escape from the earth.

Volcanologists: Life Exploring Volcanoes

geological Having to do with geology.

geologic time The time it takes for geological processes to occur. Mountain building, for example, doesn't normally happen in a couple of years. It's a process that takes millions of years.

geology The scientific study of the earth and its history.

lahar Mudflow consisting of volcanic material and water.

lava Hot, liquefied rock that comes out of a volcano and solidifies as it cools.

magma Hot, liquefied material found inside a volcano; magma is ejected from a volcano as lava and volcanic gas during an eruption.

monitor To watch, record, and keep track of.

noxious Poisonous.

pressure An expanding force that occurs when volcanic magma and gases build up beneath the earth's surface.

pyroclastic flow An avalanche of volcanic ash and rock.

rim The outer edge of a volcanic cone.

satellite A man-made object that is launched into space and that orbits the earth.

seismic activity Movements in the earth that result
   from earthquakes.

vent A break in the surface of the earth from which
   volcanic gases can escape.

volcanic Having to do with volcanoes.

volcanic cone Many volcanoes are shaped like
   cones; the cone is the volcano itself and the hole
   in the middle of the volcano.

volcanism Volcanic activity.

volcanologist A scientist who studies volcanoes.

For
More
Information

In the United States

American Geophysical Union (AGU)
2000 Florida Avenue NW
Washington, DC 20009-1277
(800) 966-2481
Web site: http://earth.agu.org

Geological Society of America
P.O. Box 9140
Boulder, CO 80301-9140

(800) 472-1988
Web site: http://www.geosociety.org

International Association of Volcanology and
　　Chemistry of the Earth's Interior (IAVCEI)
P.O. Box 185
Campbell ACT 2612
Australia
Web site: http://www.iavcei.org

U.S. Geological Survey (USGS)
National Center
12201 Sunrise Valley Drive
Reston, VA 20192
(703) 648-4000
Web site: http://www.usgs.gov

In Canada

Geological Association of Canada
Department of Earth Sciences
Alexander Murray Building, Room ER4063
Memorial University of Newfoundland
St. John's, NF A1B 3X5

Volcanologists: Life Exploring Volcanoes

(709) 737-7660
Web site: http://www.esd.mun.ca/~gac

Geological Survey of Canada
Natural Resources Canada
601 Booth Street
Ottawa, ON K1A 0E8
(613) 995-3084
Web site: http://www.nrcan.gc.ca/gsc

Web Sites

Due to the changing nature of Internet links, the Rosen Publishing Group, Inc., has developed an online list of Web sites related to the subject of this book. This site is updated regularly. Please use this link to access the list:

http://www.rosenlinks.com/eca/volc/

For Further Reading

Berger, Gilda, and Melvin Berger. *Why Do Volcanoes Blow Their Tops? Questions and Answers About Volcanoes and Earthquakes.* New York: Scholastic Reference, 2000.

Bruce, Victoria. *No Apparent Danger: The True Story of Volcanic Disaster at Galeras and Nevado del Ruiz.* New York: HarperCollins Publishers, 2001.

Fisher, Richard. *Out of the Crater: Chronicles of a Volcanologist.* Princeton, NJ: Princeton University Press, 1999.

Krafft, Maurice, and Katia Krafft. *Volcanoes: Fire from the Earth.* New York: Harry N. Abrams, Inc., 1993.

Thompson, Dick. *Volcano Cowboys: The Rocky Evolution of a Dangerous Science.* New York: St. Martin's Press, 2000.

Volcanologists: Life Exploring Volcanoes

Thompson, Luke. *Volcanoes*. Danbury, CT: Children's Press, 2000.

Van Rose, Susanna. *Eyewitness: Volcano and Earthquake*. London: DK Publishing, 2000.

Williams, Stanley, and Fen Montaigne. *Surviving Galeras*. New York: Houghton Mifflin Company, 2001.

Bibliography

International Association of Volcanology and
    Chemistry of the Earth's Interior Web site.
    Retrieved November 2001 (http://www.lavcei.org).
Krafft, Maurice, and Katia Krafft. *Volcanoes: Fire from
    the Earth*. New York: Harry N. Abrams, Inc., 1993.
Thompson, Rick. *Volcano Cowboys: The Rocky
    Evolution of a Dangerous Science*. New York:
    St. Martin's Press, 2000.
Williams, Stanley, and Fen Montaigne. *Surviving
    Galeras*. New York: Houghton Mifflin
    Company, 2001.

Index

About the Author

Chris Hayhurst is a writer who lives in Colorado.

Photo Credits

Cover and p. 35 © Roger Ressmeyer/Corbis; pp. 5, 48 © Digitalvision; p. 6 © Archivo Icon Grafico, S.A./Corbis; pp. 9, 15, 17, 42 © AP/Wide World Photos; pp. 10, 22, 38 Photo by Lynn Topinka, USGS/CVO; p. 12 Photo by Austin Post, USGS/CVO; p. 24 Photo by Eugene Y. Iwatsubo, USGS/CVO; p. 29 © AFP/Corbis; p. 33 Photo by Thomas J. Casadevall, USGS/CVO; p. 44 © Mikkel Juul Jensen/Bonnier Publications/SPL/Photo Researchers.

Design and Layout

Les Kanturek